TONY GONZALEZ

CATCH & CONNECT

Positively for Kids®
Kirkland Avenue Office Park
811 Kirkland Avenue, Suite 200
Kirkland, WA 98033
www.positivelyforkids.com

Gonzales, Tony, 1976 –
Tony Gonzalez—Catch & Connect / by Tony Gonzalez with Greg Brown.
48-p.:ill. (mostly col.), ports.; 26 cm (Positively For Kids)
Summary: Tony Gonzalez, tight end for the Kansas City Chiefs football team, recounts
his experiences growing up that have contributed to success on and off the field,
stressing that it's how one catches opportunities and stays connected to family that
ultimately determines success.
Audience: Grades 4-8

ISBN 0-9634650-8-2

I. Gonzalez, Tony, 1976 - Juvenile literature.2. Football players—United States—
Juvenile literature. [I.Gonzalez, Tony, 19 -. 2. Football players—Biography.]
I. Brown, Greg, 1957- . II. Title.

796.332/092—dc21[B]

Library of Congress Control Number:
2004110332

Photo Credits:
All photos courtesy of Tony Gonzalez and family except the following:
AP/Wide World: 31 top left; 40 top right. Darren Bennett: 47 right. Cal Media
Relations: 28 left; 31 bottom left. Kansas City Chiefs: 5 right. Keith Dannemiller: 43
left; 45. Tom Dipace: 6; 36 left; 36 top right; 40 bottom left; 46. Getty Images: 19; 29;
31 right; 34. *The Kansas City Star*: 43 right. Jack Gruber/*USA Today*: 37.
Hank Young: 35 left; 35 right; 38; 39; 40 top left; 40 middle left; 47 left.

Special Thanks:
Positively For Kids would like to thank the people and organizations that helped make
this book possible: Tony Gonzalez, his family and friends; Denise White of Entertainers
& Athletes Group; the Kansas City Chiefs; and the Shadow Buddies Foundation.

Book Design:
Methodologie, Inc., Seattle

Printed in Canada

TONY GONZALEZ

CATCH & CONNECT

BY **TONY GONZALEZ**
WITH **GREG BROWN**

A POSITIVELY FOR KIDS BOOK

Hi. I'm Tony Gonzalez.

If you've heard my name before it's probably because I play in the National Football League. I'm a tight end for the Kansas City Chiefs.

I joined the Chiefs in 1997 after playing football and basketball for the University of California Bears.

So far, my NFL career has produced memorable seasons and a few that are forgettable. I've been honored to be named an All-Pro five times. Some say my mix of size (I'm 6-foot-4, 250 pounds), speed, agility, toughness, hands, and grace make me unique for the tight end position.

A tight end is a cross between a lineman and wide receiver, with a dash of running back. I block defenders on run plays and I go out for passes. Catching passes, running the football, and scoring touchdowns are the glamour moments of my job. I also enjoy being in the trenches and slamming defenders to free our running backs. I have the best of both worlds.

The same could be said about my family. As you can see by my face, I'm a mixture of races.

YEAR 1982

YEAR 2004

My mother's family includes African Americans, Caucasians, and Native Americans. My father's heritage is Jamaican, Portuguese, and Scottish. My bloodlines are a melting pot of cultures. This has allowed me to connect with many types of people. I'm proud of all I am.

My story will give you a glimpse below my skin. You'll see I've faced the same challenges and setbacks many kids experience. I wasn't always a tough guy. In fact, there was a time when playing football frightened me. I hated the sport and wanted to quit.

I lacked confidence in junior high and the start of high school. I was kind of a geek and a coward. Girls ignored me. I experienced the pain of being bullied in eighth grade.

I've written this book to share with you the true stories of my life and perhaps change perceptions. I hope to motivate you to catch the opportunities that come your way. Above all else, I challenge you to stay connected to your loved ones and dare to connect with others.

> Mom holds me in her arms with brother Chris in tow.

> I'm screaming scared on my first horse ride.

My family connection began on February 27, 1976, my birth day. I was the second son born to Judy and Joseph Gonzalez. When I came along people thought there was something wrong with me. I always had a goofy look as a baby.

I'm told I was very active as a kid, even hyperactive. I always wanted to keep up with my brother, Chris, who is two years older. I was a big kid for my age and eventually outgrew Chris.

Mom says I reminded her of a Shepherd puppy. My body grew too fast at times, making me clumsy.

I'D BREAK THINGS JUST WALKING BY THEM BECAUSE I DIDN'T HAVE FULL COORDINATION OF MY BODY. I WAS A WALKING ACCIDENT.

Christmas tree ornaments didn't stand a chance with me. If I didn't knock them off by accident, I would often crush them while holding them. When we took them off the tree, no matter how careful I tried to be, I'd drop or break them.

For seven years our family life was stable. We had nice houses in Norwalk, Cerritos, and Long Beach, California. I learned to scuba dive in our backyard pool. Both my parents worked for different hospitals—my father in the psychiatric ward; Mom started her career as a nurse.

Unfortunately, my parents decided to divorce when I was 7. Chris and I lived with Mom, but we saw Dad regularly on the weekends. Breaking up a family is never easy. Mom struggled being a single parent. For a short time we needed the support of food stamps to keep meals on the table and we moved around before settling in Huntington Beach, California. I never realized how close to the edge we lived. Mom provided for our needs. I wore a lot of clothes from the flea market or hand-me-downs from Chris or relatives.

> Making a mess in our backyard.
> My first studio baby picture.

Mom always looked for inexpensive entertainment. A favorite family activity was going to drive-in movies. We'd pack our car with family and friends and watch outdoor movies from our car. You couldn't beat the price. We paid about 15 bucks for a full car.

Another family outing used to be watching the Formula One races at the Long Beach Grand Prix. We'd make a weekend of watching the world's fastest cars race. We still try to attend every year. It's become a family tradition.

Being a California kid, the streets and surf were always free fun. I tried skateboarding, biking, and surfing. I never had the hot boards or bikes like some of the kids. I wanted to fit in with school friends so I tried my best to be a skater. Big bodies and boards don't go together well. My knees always were scraped up. I was OK, but I could never land a kickflip.

I liked jumping curbs and riding rough with my bike. I ruined about four regular bikes because I treated them like BMXers and broke many rims. My surfing days didn't last long. I learned how to stand up and ride the waves, but a bad wipeout turned me into a bodyboarder.

> The four picture slides: My parents on their wedding day, relatives clean my shoe after I stepped in dog doo, balancing on crutches, Mom and me in happy times.

> Below, Chris and me playing around.

> Chris, right, and I were mean machines to each other.

None of the boarding and biking sent me to the hospital. I did need stitches near my ankle when I was 10. I fell running down bleachers and sliced my ankle.

I probably should have gone to the hospital the day Chris threw a rock at me from our roof. He should have been a quarterback! He hit me in the head while I was standing on our street about 40 yards away. Blood gushed out of my head. We washed the cut and stopped the bleeding in our bathroom as Chris freaked out. He thought he really hurt me this time. He also feared the consequences.

"DON'T TELL MOM, OK?" HE BEGGED ME. I DIDN'T.

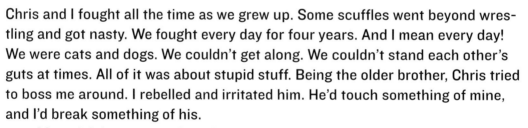

> Chris and I get dirty.
> I'm ready to hit the waves.

Chris and I fought all the time as we grew up. Some scuffles went beyond wrestling and got nasty. We fought every day for four years. And I mean every day! We were cats and dogs. We couldn't get along. We couldn't stand each other's guts at times. All of it was about stupid stuff. Being the older brother, Chris tried to boss me around. I rebelled and irritated him. He'd touch something of mine, and I'd break something of his.

Mom didn't approve of our fighting. It drove her crazy. Still, she didn't always step in to break it up. She made us work it out on our own. She knew she wouldn't always be there to stand between us.

Chris and I spent a lot of time together. With Mom working so much, Chris and I were latchkey kids during elementary school days. We spent a lot of after-school hours at the Boys & Girls Club or at home.

I SPENT HOURS SHOOTING BASKETS AT THE CITY GYM. I ENJOYED BASKETBALL MORE THAN FOOTBALL. CHRIS, HOWEVER, IS THE REASON I'M A FOOTBALL PLAYER.

> I hold a pair of candles before blowing them out.

> Chris and I take a break on a fishing trip to Mexico.

He's the one who loved football. He played Pop Warner football and got hooked. He played linebacker in high school and played a little college football at Texas A&M Commerce until a back injury ended his career.

Chris threw me my first pass at a playground near our house. He was in seventh grade, I was in fourth. He taught me how to position my hands and encouraged me to play the game. First he showed me how to catch by trapping the ball between my hands and body. Later we worked on just using my hands. We played catch a little bit every day. Despite our brotherly love-hate relationship, I always looked up to Chris and wanted to make him proud. He's the biggest reason for my football success.

As the years went by the love grew and the hate faded away. Chris is one of my best friends. We stay connected by getting together or talking by phone at least a couple times a week. I know he's got my back and I have his. I helped him cover his college bills. When he needed back surgery and didn't have insurance, I paid the $30,000 bill. So if you have a sibling you can't stand now, there's hope you can grow close and connect down the road.

> On the hiking trail.
> Practicing the piano at home.
> Dad with his sons.

Many fathers push their sons to play sports. Not mine. My dad never played sports. In fact, Chris and I were the first on either side of our family to play sports. None of my uncles did. If my parents stayed together, chances are, I wouldn't have either. That's because my father's religion frowns upon playing sports from sundown Friday to sundown Sunday.

Dad nurtured other things in us. When we spent weekends with him, we went on nature walks or visited museums. We went to so many different places in the L.A. area I could be a cultural tour guide for visitors. Dad showed us America at ground level during the summer. We'd take two-week road trips to see the wonders of our country—the Grand Canyon, the Rocky Mountains, the Mississippi, Carlsbad Caverns, and Opryland. I've seen every part of America you can think of. We'd explore museums in major cities, too.

It all rubbed off on me. It helped my spirit of diversity. I appreciate other things beside sports. I like all kinds of music from classical to hip hop. I like to read all kinds of books, especially autobiographies, motivational books, and spiritual books. I've collected quite a library of books. I love art. I love going to museums. I love nature walks.

I DIDN'T LOVE MY FIRST TASTE OF ORGANIZED SPORTS. I DREADED YOUTH FOOTBALL.

Mom says she'd drop me off at practice and I'd beat her home because I didn't want to play. Most kids worry about playing time. I prayed coaches wouldn't put me in Pop Warner games. Players on our Huntington Beach Cobra team were guaranteed six plays a game. I played the minimum six. Everyone pushed me around. I didn't like hitting others. Being bigger, I was afraid of hurting the smaller players. So I'd avoid contact and run away from the action. I complained to mom about the "turns in my stomach" from anxiety before the games. Even before my first few high school games, I'd be so stressed I secretly vowed to myself "I'm not playing next year."

I kept playing youth football without many highlights. I was the big guy who didn't play to his potential. I'm proof you can't judge your athletic future on youth sports. Some of the best youth football players didn't even play in high school. You never know how things will turn out in sports. I played youth basketball and found more success there.

The turning point in sports came for me the summer after eighth grade. I started playing summer basketball for Coach Neiderhouse. He taught me not to fear contact and showed me how to use my size on the court. I found my courage to compete.

That same year marked another crossroad. My eighth-grade year at Sowers Middle School was the worst year of my life.

I was a so-so student. I did enough to get by but that's all. Looking back, I lacked confidence in myself—as a student, as an athlete, and, most importantly, as a person. In class, I just didn't kick it into gear. I took the easy road to average.

In middle school I had a low self-image. I hid my skateboard in the bushes, then jumped on it at the end of school to get home as fast as possible. I never went to dances, didn't have girlfriends, and basically went home every day and watched TV. That made me an expert on '80s TV trivia, but left me lonely.

Two older guys made everything worse. They were in high school and came down to middle school periodically to terrorize me. They threatened me and pushed me around (even though I was a little taller than they were). They even called me at home. They kept bullying me day after day.

On my eighth-grade graduation day they came and glared at me from the audience. It scared me out of my mind. After the ceremony, I ran off and hid. "Where's Tony?" members of my family said to each other. My family didn't know where I went, so they looked around. They wanted to congratulate me and give me a hug.

Mom, Chris, aunts, uncles, cousins, and friends all found me cowering around a school building corner, my back to the wall, paralyzed with fear.

All I remember is seeing the disappointment in the eyes of Mom and Chris. They knew about the bullies. They knew I ran away from my problem. I felt so ashamed.

That moment changed my life.

I REMEMBER SAYING TO MYSELF I'LL NEVER EVER SEE THAT LOOK ON THEIR FACES AGAIN. THAT MOMENT IS WHEN I SAID I'M NOT RUNNING FROM ANYONE EVER AGAIN.

Bullying is a problem in schools. It's not always the big guys picking on the little guys. It's not always guys—girls bully too. It's about having power over someone. Those who do bully generally have been bullied themselves or have such a sorry self-image they have to boost theirs by putting others down. Bullying shows their weakness, not their strength. And some people have mean streaks. Maybe their family life is so bad, that's how they get back at the world.

What should you do if you're bullied or someone you know is? Each situation is different. When do you walk away and when do you make a stand? When do you tell a teacher, a counselor, your principal, your parents, the police? This page has some resource contacts and advice of experts. The worst thing to do is keep it to yourself. You need to talk about it with someone you trust. Decide to do something about it. Doing nothing will not make the problem go away.

BULLIES!

What is bullying?
Physical bullying hitting, kicking, stealing, or damaging property.
Verbal bullying humiliating with words by name-calling, teasing, or insulting.
Repeated teasing and cruelty of any kind.
Roughhousing when the other child or teen does not agree to it.

Who bullies?
A person who seeks power over others.
Someone who needs to feel in control of other people.
A person who does not accept responsibility for his or her actions.

Who gets bullied?
Anyone can become a victim of bullying.
Anyone who witnesses repeated bullying is affected.
Most people do not report a bully so the bullying continues.

What can I do?
Realize it is not your fault.
Inform an adult whom you trust. Adults have the power to make significant changes in kids' lives.

What do I do if a kid at school is picking on me?
Bullies usually feel badly about themselves and that's why they pick on people. Try hard not to get mad or let them provoke you. If you feel like you can handle it, try to stand tall and say, "I'm not going to fight with you." Look the bully in the eye and talk calmly. You could say "Leave me alone," or "You don't scare me." Try to not run away (unless you are being attacked).
But remember, you don't have to handle it on your own.
Your parents may be able to talk with your teacher or counselor about this if you ask them.

Strategy
Walk Walk away from the bullying child or children.
Talk Talk to the bully in a firm, confident voice. Tell them to stop and leave you alone.
Squawk After the encounter, squawk to adults about the episode. Those not involved in bullying who see another child being harmed also should seek help from an adult immediately.
You might worry about making other kids angry by telling on them, but exposing the abuse is the only way to stop the problem.

For help and information call: 1.877-KIDS-400

Sources
www.kidscrisis.com

HOWEVER YOU HANDLE IT, JUST KNOW YOU'RE NOT ALONE. AND KNOW SCHOOL DOESN'T LAST FOREVER. YOU MIGHT EVEN RUN INTO YOUR BULLIES IN THE FUTURE AND HAVE THE UPPER HAND.

Years after my incident at graduation, I ran into both guys. By that time I'd grown more and towered over both of them. Neither seemed so scary anymore. Now they were afraid of me.

One of the guys, Curtis, I saw in high school two years later. I went up to him and gave him a laugh like "You're little!" I didn't do anything. I walked right past him and brushed him.

The other, Rich, I met my senior year. I pulled into a gas station where he worked. I could see fear in his eyes.

"Aren't you Rich?" I said. "What's up, do you remember me?"

"I remember you," he said in a shaky voice.

"What are you doing these days," I said.

"Nothing," Rich answered. "We're cool, right?"

"Relax," I said. "I'm not going to do anything."

And I didn't. My revenge came by facing both of them down without fear.

> Michael, my stepdad (center), with cousin Dennis (left), Travis, and Vince, who lived with us as brothers.

> Travis, Chris, Vince, Donnie, me, and childhood friend Mike celebrate at Vince's wedding.

> Our diverse family blends nicely together on Chris's graduation day from college.

Mom was proud when I told her how I handled the situations. She had taught us all about compassion through her career in health care and by opening our home to others. By the time I reached high school, I had three brothers.

Through the years we crossed paths with friends who had rough family lives. Young men and women whose family lives were so bad they couldn't, or didn't want to, live at their homes anymore. Despite our tight money, Mom invited them to stay with us.

Space and food became an issue. I slept on a body-width ledge above our bedroom closet for three years to make enough room for our growing family. To keep a handle on the food, Mom placed a lock on our refrigerator and pantry and limited what we could eat when she wasn't home. I figured out how to unscrew the refrigerator and pantry handles to open the doors. I got caught when I left dishes in my bedroom.

Mom went back to school and earned a degree in administration and is an administrator for a nursing home. She remarried when I was 13 and Michael Saltzman has been a wonderful stepdad. I can't say enough about the sacrifices Mom made for us.

These days, Mom and Michael host Sunday barbecues for our extended family. If you came to one you'd find a rainbow of races in our house. If it's football season, they watch my games and celebrate the victories and scream at the TV when I make a mistake.

When I started high school I still wasn't sure if playing football was a mistake for me. I had the size, but didn't have that aggressive spirit. I played for the freshman team that year.

ONE PLAY OPENED MY EYES TO MY POTENTIAL. I BLEW OVER A SMALLER DEFENDER ON MY WAY TO A TOUCHDOWN. THE LIGHT WENT ON IN MY HEAD AND I REALIZED HOW TO USE MY SIZE.

I had a great season. My sophomore year, three in my class were called up to play varsity. I was the last of the three to be brought up and eventually showed what I could do.

The Huntington Beach football program didn't have much respect around the league. The Oilers had not been to the playoffs in more than 10 years. But my junior and senior years we had a great group of athletes and our team jelled.

My junior and senior years we won league championships in football and basketball. We were unchallenged in our league.

After a solid junior football season, I entered my senior year as an All-County pick. I played my worst varsity game the opening contest of the season. We beat Downey 28-0 but I had only two catches the whole night and no touchdowns.

My best game came against Marina High. I had four touchdowns in the first half, three with receptions. We ran the table, going 13-0 before losing in the CIF state playoffs to Los Alamitos, ranked 25th in the country.

I set a few school records with 62 catches for 945 yards and 13 touchdowns. I also played linebacker on defense, and I led our team on tackles with 131. No longer afraid of contact, I loved tackling. Only a handful of players make the High School All-America team. I was voted on the first team for both offense and defense.

On the basketball court, we were ranked 35th in the country at one point my senior year. We competed well against national powers Mater Dei and Oak Hill Academy. We finished fourth in our state tournament, losing to Crenshaw 61-58. It's amazing what we accomplished.

The Orange County & Sunset League coaches voted me the Most Valuable Player as I averaged 26 points a game on 65 percent shooting.

My success in sports brought me out of my social shell. I made tight friends and caught the eye of girls. I think my early lack of success in sports and awkwardness in middle school kept me humble when I became accepted with the "cool" crowd. I was able to keep it in perspective. I never thought I was too cool. I tried not to be a jerk. I never ever made fun of people.

Huntington Beach has many wealthy families. You'd see school kids driving BMWs and Porsches to school. To some, their clothes and car defines their status. I didn't care much about that stuff.

I was happy just to have wheels. I drove a rusty orange Volkswagen Bug to school every day. The 1972 VW used to be Chris's and was passed down to me.

There was no back seat. Wear and tear exposed wires through the back-seat cloth. Nothing worked. The windows didn't roll down. They were frozen halfway down all the time. When I stepped on the brakes and came to a stop, the engine shut off. I'd have to restart the car. No tunes. The radio didn't work. Plus, the engine was real loud. "Tony's here," my friends would say when I was still a block away.

College coaches and recruiters knew where to find me. I got offers to play at 80 Division I schools. My decision came down to Cal, Arizona, Florida State,

> Chris and I squeeze into his VW Bug.

> I accept the Orange County MVP Trophy at a basketball game.

> Can you find me in my high school basketball team photo?

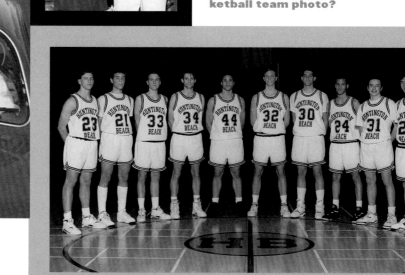

Notre Dame, Washington and Colorado, all of which recruited me to play both sports. I picked the Cal Bears.

That spring two memorable things happened—memorable for completely different reasons.

The *Orange County Register* newspaper picked two high school Athletes of the Year in 1994—me and this other guy, a golfer. I remember hearing that name and saying, "Who? Who is this guy with the weird name?" I was like, a golfer for Athlete of the Year?

So the newspaper hosts a big banquet every year to honor all the area's high school sports stars. The golfer never showed up. I thought, "A golfer, and he doesn't show up for the awards ceremony. Who does he think he is?"

APPARENTLY, TIGER WOODS WAS PLAYING IN SOME GOLF TOURNAMENT AND COULDN'T ATTEND. I'VE STILL NEVER MET TIGER, BUT SOMEWHERE A TROPHY HAS BOTH OF OUR NAMES ON IT.

HIGH SCHOOL HIGHLIGHTS

FOOTBALL

YR	Rec	Yds	TD
Senior	62	945	13

All-State selection as tight end and linebacker

BASKETBALL

YR	PPG	FGP	MS/AS
Senior	26.0	65%	234/365

MVP of Orange County & Sunset League

Co-Athlete of the Year of Orange County with Tiger Woods

> Travis and me hanging
out after a high school
practice. Sometimes
we'd hit the beach after
football practices.

> Chris and I suddenly
find ourselves taller
than our father.

> Mom and me at my
high school graduation.

The top senior football players were invited at the end of the school year to play an All-Star game. I only survived one play.

On my first play, I caught a pass and someone tackled me. A lightning bolt shot through my right knee.

IT FELT SERIOUS. THEY STOPPED THE GAME AND GOT A STRETCHER AND AMBULANCE. I HAD NEVER BEEN HURT IN ANY OF MY PREVIOUS HIGH SCHOOL GAMES. I DIDN'T KNOW WHAT WAS GOING ON.

Then Nick Ziggler, a close friend, came over and looked at my twisted leg. Then the All-Star coaches knelt down next to me. It terrified me. Seeing the look on their faces is what scared me. I knew it was bad.

I held it together until I got in the ambulance. Then I started crying, all the way to the hospital. My mind started going dark. Was this my last football game ever? Would I be able to run again? Is my basketball career over?

At the hospital a friend's dad, Dr. Reynolds, gave me comfort. He worked in the sports department. He told me I was going to be OK. That settled me down.

The news wasn't so bad. I sprained my medial collateral ligament—MCL for short. It could've been much worse. I didn't need surgery, but I rehabbed the whole summer to be ready for football in the fall at Cal.

The scare was a reminder that sports and your health can be taken away in a flash. We do need to catch and treasure every day, every opportunity.

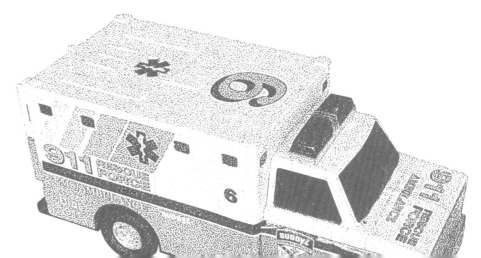

Going to college is a great opportunity for anyone. I spent three years at Berkeley, across the bay from San Francisco. Looking back, I can say my time in college was one of the best investments of my time. It made me who I am today. Interacting with different groups, exercising my mind, competing at a high level, and dealing with the world on my own taught invaluable lessons.

My first few years at Cal caused growing pains. It was the first time I was away from home for an extended time. Growing up in Huntington Beach, I hung around with a mixture of people. At Cal most of the athletes were black. I feel comfortable with all groups of people, but not everyone is comfortable with me.

Sometimes I got it from all sides. In high school, we had skinheads to deal with. I heard the word "nigger" many times. It's a word you don't ignore when it's said in hate, but you learn to live with it. A Mexican gang once gave me a little verbal trouble. At Cal, some of the black athletes questioned my Beach upbringing.

One called me an Uncle Tom. That's a term used for African Americans who "act white." I was just acting like myself.

I DIDN'T HAVE ALL THE STREET SLANG AND THEY SAID I SOUNDED TOO WHITE. I'D HATE TO CALL IT AN IDENTITY CRISIS—JUST GROWING INTO MY OWN SKIN.

I also learned about sports corruption. Our Bears basketball coach was fired my sophomore year for breaking NCAA recruiting rules. It didn't surprise me. I had heard stories. I didn't like his coaching style anyway, so I welcomed the change. A dark cloud of suspicion shadowed all of us.

When the scandal broke, everyone assumed I was paid off too.

"Tony, how much did you get?" people asked me. Some still ask about it.

The truth is I didn't get anything extra. One of my best friends, and college roommate at the time, got tangled in the mess and didn't even know it. His father took cash without his knowledge. The player eventually transferred to another school. The experience showed me how money can stain sports. In the pros, sports is all business. Everyone knows it. But in college it's not about who's making what. That's why I enjoyed playing at Cal, especially my final year.

MY BASKETBALL SEASONS AT CAL STARTED SLOWLY. IT TOOK ME SOME TIME TO GET INTO BASKETBALL SHAPE. ONE YEAR I PLAYED IN THE FINAL CAL FOOTBALL GAME OF THE SEASON AND THEN PLAYED IN AN EXHIBITION BEARS BASKETBALL GAME THAT SAME NIGHT.

So my three seasons of basketball, I played only a few minutes a game the first half of the season and then I'd come on strong at the end.

When new coach Ben Braun took over, basketball became fun again. Many NFL scouts and some coaches watched me play basketball to gauge my football potential. My junior year, Ed Gray emerged as the team leader. He became the Pac-10 Player of the Year. We made the NCAA playoffs, but we lost him to injury in our last six games of the year. I stepped in and my average went up from 3 to 18 points per game.

A dramatic game for me was on national TV. We played Alabama in a tight game. We were down by one point, and I was fouled with no time on the clock. If I missed we'd lose. I made the first free throw to guarantee overtime. They called time out and cleared the free-throw line. I was out there by myself with a chance to win it. I barely missed. We lost in overtime. My brother, Chris, just says "Alabama" whenever he wants to tease me.

In the NCAA tournament we advanced to the Sweet 16, thanks to a win over Princeton in the first round. Again, I went to the free-throw line with the game on the line. They fouled me twice in a row down the stretch. I hit both the first time and 1-of-2 on the second to protect our lead. That was clutch for me to perform under pressure. Reporters voted me Player of the Game.

I went into college football as a highly touted recruit. But I didn't live up to my hype at first. My first two years of football at Cal I didn't do anything great until the last game of my sophomore year.

My freshman year I felt the burden of making a game-losing fumble against Washington State. I caught a pass in the closing minutes and fumbled. That allowed WSU to score the winning field goal.

After everyone cleared out of our locker room, I sat there with all my gear still on and cried my brains out. My coach, Keith Gilbertson, came over and gave me a hug and said "Don't worry, you have a great future ahead of you."

One of my best friends in the world, Deana Itow, helped me through that period and many others. Deana was my girlfriend in high school and much of college. She played college basketball and knows everything about sports. Even though we broke up we've remained close friends.

The big rivalry game every year is against Stanford, in the final regular-season game. They call it the "Big Game." It's one of the oldest college football rivalries,

> Cal teammates and I relax before playing in the Aloha Bowl.

dating back to 1892. My freshman year, in 1994, we won. I didn't play. The next two years we lost, one thanks to me.

My sophomore season I didn't do much until that final game against Stanford. It marked one of my best and worst games at Cal.

My 10 catches for 150 yards and one touchdown ranked as the second-best day for a Cal tight end. But one catch ended just like the WSU game the year before. With nine minutes to play, we trailed 23-17 but were driving toward a score. I caught a pass in the flat and turned it up field and got nailed by a tackler. I thought I was down before the ball popped loose. The referees ruled otherwise. Stanford took over and scored in four plays to seal our 29-23 loss.

Despite the outcome, my performance in that game gave me something to build on.

THE NEXT YEAR THINGS CHANGED FOR ME AT SCHOOL. I STARTED FOCUSING MORE. I WORKED HARDER.

My junior season we went 6-5, and NFL scouts took notice of my numbers. Reporters started asking me, "So are you going to come out after your junior year?"

"What are you talking about?" I said.

"Are you going to declare yourself eligible for the draft?"

"What are you talking about, the NFL draft?" I said with almost a laugh. "No, I haven't thought about it."

Until reporters asked me, the idea of being drafted never even crossed my mind. It was never about going to the NFL for me. A lot of kids today come up and say, "Oh, I'm going to the big leagues." I never made such predictions. I didn't dare look that far ahead while in college. My goals were to be the best I could today and let tomorrow take care of itself.

After the season a few honors came my way. I made the first team All-America college football team and there was a buzz about going high in the draft. I decided to give the NFL a try. The door was open, it was time to walk though and catch this chance.

My parents joined me at the 1997 draft. It was crazy. The Kansas City Chiefs picked me lucky 13th overall. Going with Kansas City (KC) excited me. Elvis Grbac and Rich Gannon were the quarterbacks and coach Marty Schottenheimer ran the West Coast offense, in which tight ends have many opportunities to catch passes.

My NFL career, so far, has been like being on a teeter-totter. There have been up and downs. Seems God has a way of keeping me humble and level-headed. As soon as I thought "I'm the man," something happened.

Plus, I have a great family that can build me up when I'm down or keep me grounded and never let me get cocky.

MY ROOKIE YEAR WENT LIKE A DREAM. I GOT TO PLAY RIGHT AWAY AS A BACKUP. LED BY MARCUS ALLEN, WE WON THE AFC WEST TITLE WITH A 13-3 RECORD. WE LOST TO DENVER IN THE PLAYOFFS. MAKING THE PLAY-OFFS IN MY ROOKIE SEASON MADE IT SEEM EASY. BUT OUR TEAM WOULDN'T TASTE THE PLAYOFFS FOR FIVE FRUSTRATING YEARS.

The next season I struggled as a starter. I dropped 17 passes. Our 7-9 record disappointed all of us. A sportswriter graded my year as a D-minus. I'd never received a D in anything, school or sports. People stopped me on the street and asked: "What's wrong?" I didn't have an answer. I worked very hard to prepare for the season and had nothing to show for it. I showed my frustrations. I'd pick up a dropped ball and slam it to the ground. I was pressing.

> Chris, my big sister and manager Denise White, and me.

About that time, my really good friend Donnie Berger sent me a letter of encouragement and book of quotes by Vince Lombardi. That started me reading inspirational books. I read motivational books by Pat Riley, Phil Jackson, Lou Holtz, Tony Robbins, and others. I enjoy reading biographies of successful people.

By the end of the season things started to click. The last five games I played well. That gave me a comfort level. Just like in high school and college, my third year became my breakout.

The 1999 season I led all KC receivers in receptions (76) and was named to my first Pro Bowl. The 11 touchdowns rank as my career high for the season, so far.

SPEAKING OF TOUCHDOWNS, I LIKE TO "DUNK" THE FOOTBALL THROUGH THE GOAL POSTS WHENEVER I SCORE. THAT'S MY LITTLE TRIBUTE TO THE GAME OF BASKETBALL.

The problem with success in the NFL is teams find a way to stop you. The next season teams started to double- and triple-team me. Still, Grbac managed to find me 93 times in 2000 for 1,203 yards, both of which were most in a season for me. Dick Vermeil took over the head coaching duties in 2001 and our offense changed.

My involvement changed and I wasn't happy about it. They weren't throwing to me as much. I worried about my statistics. I went to the media and said I wanted the ball. We were 3-8 at one point, and I thought I could help more.

Parts of that season felt unbearable. One of the hardest things in sports is to lose like that. We couldn't put it together. We put everything into it. When you put your heart into it, you try to prepare yourself the best you can, and you still come up short, you still can't win, that tests your determination.

Looking back, complaining about my stats was a selfish thing to do. The statistic that means the most is wins and losses. We missed the playoffs again at 6-10.

I finally figured out it's more important for me to go out and help the team do well than go out and worry about my own statistics. If I don't have catches, so be it. That's fine. That change of attitude has made all the difference. Football became fun again.

SIDELINE INJURIES

One of the strangest things to happen in a football game took place Nov. 11, 2000, in San Francisco.

I caught a pass and a linebacker shoved me out of bounds. I accidentally crashed into a 51-year-old photographer on the sidelines named Mickey Pfleger.

The blow knocked Mickey unconscious and he went into a seizure. He had this dazed look. He started shaking. I was still trying to talk to him, "Are you all right? Are you all right?" And he didn't answer me.

I've hit people on the sideline before, and usually they get right up. I was expecting him to get up, and I was going to help him up. But I looked at his eyes, and they were rolled back. The next thing I know, the ref is pulling me away, saying I needed to get to the huddle. It was terrible. Everyone thought he was seriously hurt.

Pfleger was taken to a hospital by ambulance. Doctors found no serious injuries. They did a brain scan because of the seizure.

The test revealed a brain tumor, which doctors removed. Turns out, our "connection" was a blessing in disguise and saved his life.

I sent some flowers and a football to Mickey's home when he got out of the hospital with a note that said: "I am so sorry about our unfortunate meeting. I truly hope you are OK and doing well. Please keep us updated on your condition."

Contract negotiations between a team and a player are never fun. Talks on my contract extension dragged on and on into the summer camp. As the 2002 season neared, team president Carl Peterson asked me to come back and promised to give me a fair deal. I believed him and came back. With four days' practice, I played in our first game against Cleveland and caught the first TD of the season in a win.

THAT NEXT WEEK PETERSON KEPT HIS WORD AND WE AGREED TO A SEVEN-YEAR DEAL. MY FEELING IS IF YOU CAN'T TRUST YOUR BOSS, IT'S TIME TO FIND ANOTHER ONE.

We improved to 8-8 as running back Priest Holmes started lighting it up and doing well for us.

I really thought 2003 would be our year to win the Super Bowl. With Holmes churning on the ground with an NFL-record 27 touchdowns and quarterback Trent Green passing well, we cruised through the regular season to finish with a 13-3 record. We were unbeaten at home, where we hosted Indianapolis in the divisional playoffs. Despite Holmes' team playoff-record 176 rushing yards, Colt QB Peyton Manning's 304 passing yards and three touchdowns ended our season in a 38-31 loss.

After such a spectacular regular season, not making it to the Super Bowl was extremely hard on all of us connected to the Chiefs and all our fans. We all put our souls into it. When it didn't work out, it crushed us.

So the pain lasts a while. Soon, however, it eases. You move on and look forward. You go back to work. You start to believe again. My family helps me keep such losses in perspective—especially my son Nikko. Even though things didn't work out between his mother and me and we decided not to marry, we realized neither of us could run from our responsibilities with Nikko. We've remained friends and work together to raise Nikko. Making a baby doesn't make you a man—putting in the time and effort to care for one does. Nikko has given me a whole new perception of life and has showed me the true meaning of unconditional love.

FUN FACT >>> TONY WRITES HIS TEAM'S NAME ON HIS RIGHT FOREARM, HIS BROTHER'S INITIALS CG ABOVE, AND HIS SON'S INITIALS BELOW, AND KISSES ALL THREE FOR LUCK BEFORE THE START OF A GAME OR WHEN THE TEAM IS LOSING.

41

During my time in Kansas City, I've done my best to connect with the community. I've been involved in over 100 charity events throughout the years. When fans want to talk, I do my best to share myself.

The last several years many Hispanic kids have come up to me and fired off questions in Spanish. Up until recently, my response has been "Lo siento no hablo," which means "Sorry, I don't understand."

With my last name, it's been embarrassing not to know Spanish.

SO DURING THE SPRING OF 2004 I DID SOMETHING ABOUT THAT. I WENT TO SCHOOL. I ENROLLED IN AN INTENSIVE SPANISH-LANGUAGE PROGRAM IN SAN MIGUEL DE ALLENDE, MEXICO.

I moved there for four weeks. I studied Spanish six hours a day, five days a week. The rest of the time I lived with a local family, none of whom spoke English. The class cost me $4,000. I gave up a $150,000 bonus for missing workouts in Kansas City. That's how badly I wanted to learn.

I took Spanish in middle and high school (sadly, I didn't do too well). I didn't care then. Before these classes in Mexico, however, I felt as nervous as I do before games. The mind games were intense.

One day, before I could speak Spanish well, I came across a young boy in the street wearing my Kansas City football jersey. I excitedly went up and pointed to "Gonzalez" on his back and then pointed to myself. He didn't see the connection. He didn't know my face or anything about me. The only thing that mattered to him was the Hispanic name on the jersey.

Day by day, my thinking started to shift. The puzzle of a new language came together. New words started to flow and make sense.

I made my share of embarrassing mistakes. Like the time I walked a cobblestone street and tripped. I shouted what I thought meant "I fall." The people gave me an odd stare. What I really said translates to "I go to the bathroom."

Another time I made the mistake of dunking on one of the locals in a pickup basketball game. They then fouled me every time I went up and down the court.

Besides the language, the experience of being in another country is always enlightening. You see that despite the differences, people are basically the same, no matter the skin color or country. We all have a need to connect with each other.

I look forward to using my newfound language skills to converse more with my Spanish-speaking friends and fans. I'll use my education to adapt to whatever audience I find myself.

This is an important skill in whatever country you live. If you want more than minimum-wage jobs, learning to speak well is a good investment.

There's nothing wrong with changing your speech to fit your needs. That's not selling out your heritage. It's enhancing yourself.

Knowing a language isn't enough. There are variations. I can speak "street," sound "suburban," and connect in "business English." I change it up.

If I went for a job interview or a business meeting, I'm not going to sit there and say, "What's up, dog! Yeah, you know what I'm saying ..."

I'm not going to talk slang with them. That would be stupid.

If I went to the 'hood or the barrio (as they call the inner-city neighborhood in Spanish), I wouldn't talk all professional. It's all about what's your environment. But you need to have the verbal knowledge to have the options.

If you're in school, take advantage of your chances. If you're out of school, you're never too old to be a lifelong learner.

> Professor Elvira Sierra tests my Spanish speaking skills in San Miguel De Allende, Mexico.

> I tell a group of young fans about the Shadow Buddies program.

Sometimes we don't realize the most significant opportunities we have until they are gone. Only years later we discover we missed our chance.

Use the talent God has given you. Don't waste it. Catch your chances in life. Run with them toward your goal line.

And when you do drop the ball (everyone does) know that failure isn't fatal. Failure to try is.

Through your ups and downs, your connections will get you through. Be there for your family and your family will be there for you. If your family is broken, try to heal it. If it's lost, reach out and find another, just like my "brothers" found ours.

Great victories are never guaranteed. That's the thrill. And what's the gain if there is no one to share them with? If you want to be a champion in life, catch and connect.

CAL BEARS

Football

YR	NO	YDS	AVG	TD	LG
94	8	62	7.8	1	14
95	37	341	14.6	2	50
96	44	699	15.9	5	44
ALL	89	1302	12.8	8	50

Basketball

YR	G	Starts	PPG	Reb
ALL	82	16	6.4	4.3

YEARLY STATS
FOR THE KANSAS CITY CHIEFS

YR	G	Rec	Yds	Y/G	Avg	Lng	YAC	1stD	TD	Fum
97	16	33	368	23	11.2	30	4.5	21	2	0
98	16	59	621	38.8	10.5	32	3.9	33	2	3
99	15	76	849	56.6	11.2	73	3.7	47	11	2
00	16	93	1203	75.2	12.9	39	3.9	66	9	0
01	16	73	917	57.3	12.6	36	3.5	19	6	0
02	16	63	773	48.3	12.3	42	4.3	39	7	0
03	16	71	916	57.3	12.9	67	4.9	48	10	0
ALL	111	468	5647	50.9	12.1	73	4.0	303	47	5

CHARITY

Among the charity work I'm involved with, I have a special place in my heart for the people who need hospitals and those who work there.

With my parents working in hospitals, I was around them all the time. Mom found jobs for me, from mopping the floors to being an activities director for elderly folks during my junior year in high school. I played cards with them, organized trips, and just hung out and talked with them. It was fun. It helped me not feel so uncomfortable around people.

A nursing home has a mix of people. Some are bitter old people who don't want to talk to you. I'd have to go talk to them. It forced me to get over my anxiety of talking to and meeting people.

One program I'm especially close to is called "Shadow Buddies." These are dolls, specific to certain illnesses, that are given to kids in hospitals and the elderly to provide a little comfort.

The Shadow Buddies organization designed a set of dolls in my likeness. Since 1998 about 8,500 of those dolls have been given out at 50 venues through money provided from my foundation. I personally have handed out about half of those dolls through visits to children's hospitals and nursing homes.

The mission of the Tony Gonzalez Foundation is to provide emotional and educational support by helping medically challenged children through the Shadow Buddies Foundation, and providing support for the disadvantaged youth through The Boys & Girls Club.

Through my own personal experience, I fully understand the importance of building a lifelong foundation for understanding, tolerance, and compassion.

In my opinion, you're more successful, and you have a better time, when you're trying to help people around you. When you reach out to connect, it improves the world around you and is personally rewarding.

You can learn more about Shadow Buddies and my foundation at www.shadowbuddies.org.

Index

Accomplishments
  All-Pro, named five times, 4
  All-American, college, 33
  Climbing Mt. Whitney, 16
  High School Athlete of the Year, 25
  NCAA Player of the Game, 31
  Spanish, learning, 42-43
Activities
  BMX biking, 12
  Drive-in movies, 12
  Scuba diving, 9
  Surfing, 12
  Skateboarding, 12
Allen, Marcus, 35
Basketball teams
  Summer youth teams, 17
  University of California Bears, 25, 30
Being clumsy, 8-9
Books, favorite
  Autobiographies, 16
  Motivational books, 16
  Spiritual books, 16
Bullying, responding to the problem of, 18-19, 20
Cars, 24
Charity
  "Shadow Buddies," 47
  Tony Gonzalez Foundation, 47
Character trait
  Courage to compete, 17
Dealing with divorce, 9
Overcoming
  Anxiety, 17
  Being bullied, 18
  Low self-image, 18
  Racism, 28
Coaches
  Keith Gilbertson (college), 32
  Dick Vermeil (Kansas City Chiefs), 37
Corruption in sports, 30
"Dunking the football," 36, 38, 39
Family
  Chris (brother), 8-9, 13, 14, 15, 18, 24, 26, 30, 36

Judy (mom), 8, 12, 18, 20, 26
  Becoming a nurse, 21
Joseph (dad), 8, 12, 16, 18, 26
Michael Saltzman (stepdad), 20, 21
Nikko (son), 40, 41
Extended family, 21
  Denise, 36
  Dennis, 20
  Donnie, 20, 36
  Travis, 20
  Vince, 20
Football teams
  Huntington Beach Cobras, 17
  Sowers Middle School, 18
  Huntington Beach Oilers, 23
  All-County pick, 23
  All-American Team member, 23
  University of California Bears, 4, 24-25
  Rivalry with Stanford, 32
Kansas City Chiefs, 4, 35, 36, 37
Formula One racing, 12
Gray, Ed (Pac-10 Player of the Year), 30
Green, Trent (QB KC Chiefs), 41
Huntington Beach, California, 10, 17, 28
Injuries
  Being hit with a rock, 13
  MCL (medial collateral ligament), 27
  Sideline injuries, 37
Jackson, Phil, 36
Manning, Peyton (QB Indianapolis Colts), 41
Multiracial background, 7, 28
NFL draft, 33, 34
Pfleger, Mickey, 37
Pop Warner youth football, 15, 17
Positions
  Tight end, 4
Poverty, growing up with, 21
Religion, 16, 35, 44
Riley, Pat, 36
Robbins, Tony, 36
Statistics, 4, 23, 25, 33, 35, 36, 37, 41
Super Bowl, 41
Vacations, 16
Woods, Tiger, 25

Websites for Tony Gonzalez

Tony Gonzalez Foundation	http://tonygonzalezfoundation.shadowbuddies.com
National Football League (NFL)	www.nfl.com
Official NFL site for Kids	www.playfootball.com
Kansas City Chiefs	www.kcchiefs.com
Shadow Buddies	www.shadowbuddies.org
Boys & Girls Clubs of America	www.bgca.org
Reading is Fundamental	www.rif.org